Out of

Neil I

C000255739

methuen | drama

LONDON • NEW YORK • OXFORD • NEW DELHI • SYDNEY

METHUEN DRAMA
Bloomsbury Publishing Plc
50 Bedford Square, London, WC1B 3DP, UK
1385 Broadway, New York, NY 10018, USA
29 Earlsfort Terrace, Dublin 2, Ireland

BLOOMSBURY, METHUEN DRAMA and the Methuen
Drama logo are trademarks of Bloomsbury Publishing Plc

First published in Great Britain 2024

A catalogue record for this book is available from the British Library.

A catalog record for this book is available from the Library of Congress.

ISBN: PB: 978-1-3504-7682-0
ePDF: 978-1-3504-7683-7
eBook: 978-1-3504-7684-4

Series: Modern Plays

Typeset by Mark Heslington Ltd, Scarborough, North Yorkshire
Printed and bound in Great Britain

To find out more about our authors and books visit
www.bloomsbury.com and sign up for our newsletters.

Out of Season was first performed at Hampstead Theatre Downstairs, London, on 16 February 2024. The cast was as follows:

Amy	**Catrin Aaron**
Holly	**Kerry Bennett**
Chris	**Peter Bramhill**
Dev	**Neil D'Souza**
Michael	**James Hillier**

Writer	Neil D'Souza

Director	Alice Hamilton
Designer	Janet Bird
Lighting	Matt Haskins
Sound	Harry Blake
Intimacy and Movement Director	Sarah Daukes

Out of Season is a T. S. Eliot Foundation commission.

Out of Season

Characters

Chris, *white, forty-nine, male*
Dev, *British Asian, fifty, male*
Holly, *mixed-race black, thirty-seven, female*
Amy, *white, forty-five, female*
Michael, *white, fifty, male*

Songs

The Academic song (Act One Scene Two) was written by Matt Sutton.

'Out of Season' (Act Two Scene One) was written by Gil Cang, Matt Sutton and Neil D'Souza.

All other songs (except 'The House of the Rising Sun') by Neil D'Souza.

Act One

Scene One

Early evening. Late October. A two-star hotel room in semi-darkness. Third floor. Somewhat basic. It's not been updated in at least a decade, though there have been stabs at modernisation: an air-con unit replacing an old ceiling fan, the remnants of which still hang. Behind the bed, some cheap imitation art on the wall: a Picasso print. The room also contains a king size double bed, a table, a chair, a luggage rack, a grey stone floor and upstage right a large somewhat grand though dingy brown wardrobe, out of place, from a bygone era, the door of which, slightly ajar, reveals a murky interior.

Downstage right leads to the hall outside, downstage left to an offstage bathroom, and upstage left to a red-tiled sunlit balcony, below which, out of view, are a terrace, pool, busy road, beach and finally the sea.

Outside we hear the hum of traffic and a babble of voices.

A sound of a key in a lock. **Chris** *enters excitedly carrying a tiny backpack, guitar case, and a supermarket shopping bag. He is forty-nine, red-haired, from Hull, dressed in shorts, shacket (shirt/ jacket) and flip-flops. He pulls back the curtains, chuckling to himself, surveying the room, touching the walls, the floor, even looking under the bed, then at the view, before heading off to the bathroom (offstage), returning to sit on the chair and finally clocking the wardrobe.*

After a minute **Dev** *struggles in with an oversized suitcase, overstuffed backpack. He is fifty, British Asian, wearing light trousers, light cotton shirt, light summer jacket. In one hand he clutches a bottle of Spanish mineral water and in the other a copy of* Death in Venice and Other Stories *by Thomas Mann.*

Chris (*upbeat, excited*)   They've repainted . . . New bathroom. Air-con. Wardrobe's the same.

Dev   Is it?

Chris   Same view.

Dev *looks out of the window.*

Chris   Except the beach seems longer.

Dev   How does that work?

Chris   Dunno.

Dev   Double bed.

Chris   King size – this is deluxe room now, Prof.

Dev   It's a double bed, Chris.

Chris   Don't panic. It's two singles – fella said you can push 'em apart.

He takes his guitar out of the case.

Dev *tries to swing his suitcase onto the luggage rack. After two unsuccessful attempts he holds his back.*

Dev   I need pills.

Chris   Easy, tiger.

Dev   For my back. In the stress of leaving I forgot them . . .

Chris   I may have some Nurofen.

He takes out the guitar.

I'd say lugging that thing ain't too good for it.

Dev   I couldn't even fit my underwear into yours.

Chris   Don't bring any. Buy local, chuck 'em away at the end.

Dev   Nice. (*Beat.*) Do you really want to spend your birthday here?

Chris   Room 547 . . .

Chris/Dev   Stairway to heaven.

Chris *strums some upbeat chords.*

On his third attempt, **Dev** *gets the suitcase onto the rack. Then he goes back and sits on the bed, from where he clocks the wardrobe.*

Dev   The wardrobe . . . didn't you guys lock me in there?

Chris   Did we . . .?

Dev   These places . . . the mice in their million hordes.

Chris   I like it.

Dev (*noticing the print*)   There's a Picasso on the wall.

Chris   It's a deluxe room now, pal.

Dev   Is the bathroom clean?

Chris   I stashed all the booze in there for old time's sake.

Dev   And Mr Hennessey?

Chris   D'ya not see the WhatsApp?

Dev   No.

Chris   Picture of us in Manumission '95. You've got your shirt off.

Dev   Let's have a look.

Chris   On a podium, on a pill no doubt.

He shows **Dev** *the picture on his phone.*

Dev   Oh God, I look insane!

Chris   You were. We all were. It were great.

Dev   What's he saying then?

Chris   Something's come up.

Dev   Of course it has.

Chris   No, he is coming. He's flying out later with Dave Drexler.

Dev   Wow!

Chris   Dave's looking for writers to work with, so Michael's gonna hook us up . . . He was gonna bring him to one of my gigs a couple of months ago, but then they both had to suddenly fly out . . . LA.

Beat.

Raised voices from down below, a smash, an eruption of laughter, a cheer. **Chris** *checks out what's going on.*

Dev   Party's started.

Chris   It's that lot from the lobby.

They peer over the balcony.

Chris   One of 'em's quite fit actually . . . with the tats.

Dev   Bit young.

Chris   Nah.

Dev   Twenty-three, twenty-four?

Chris   Late twenties I'd say. Thirties even.

Dev   What would you even do with a girl like that?

Chris   You seriously asking me that question?

Dev   I had a girl like that in my car last week.

Chris   Oh yeah . . .?

Dev   Penny – Michael's Penny. Bumped into her in a bar in East London. She was shouting in my ear about a postgrad – wrecked – so I offered a lift home. On the way she says she's hungry, so we stop at a chicken shop and I buy her some, and she's stuffing her face, grease everywhere, and telling me about her issues with her dad and how music has literally saved her life . . . and we get to her flat and we stay in the car for ages . . . like ages . . . like forty-five minutes talking and talking . . . and then she says her flatmates are out and would I like to come in for a drink . . .

Chris   And did you?

Dev   No.

Chris   Why not?

Dev   She's Michael's daughter.

Chris   If she's up for it?

Dev   No! Besides I'm old.

Chris   Don't be daft.

Dev   After fifty, according to Hindu scriptures, one should retire from sex and family life, renounce material values and conserve the energy of the body for meditation and the greater good.

Chris   We have got to get you laid.

Dev   Too old.

Chris   Shut up about being old, will ya?

Dev   I'm exhausted in my soul.

Chris   It's yer arsehole I'm talking about. A Rula Lenska?

Dev   Sorry?

Chris   Would you like a Rula Lenska?

Dev   What you on about?

Chris   You know . . . whisky, tonic, dash of orange.

Dev   No, thank you.

Chris   It was our holiday drink, remember? Cos some knob'ead picked up tonic at duty free instead of ginger ale, so Michael made us whisky and tonics and added the orange.

Dev   Why did we call it a Rula Lenska?

Chris   Fuck knows. Want one?

Dev   No.

Chris *goes into the bathroom to make the drink.*

From below there is another eruption of laughter and some raised voices. **Dev** *peers down at them.*

Dev   They're having fun round that pool.

Chris   I bet.

Dev   Why do they do it?

Chris   Eh?

Dev   Sit around the pool when the sea's a hundred yards away?

Chris   Dunno.

Dev   But the sea's just there. It's just there. And just a few miles up the road they'd find a nice hotel with a rooftop bar.

Chris   Double the price.

Dev   I don't think it's about the money.

Chris   What's it about then?

Dev   It's what they think they deserve.

Chris   Careful.

Dev   They'll probably spend double the room rent on sambuca.

Chris   He's sounding like a Tory now.

Dev   I'm not a Tory. A Tory would cheer on their Great British values, while secretly despising them. I'm kind of . . . openly despising them.

Chris   When the revolution comes, my friend, your name is on my list.

Dev   The revolution came. We lost.

Chris (*returns with drink, peers over balcony*)   It's what Brits do on holiday: smoke, drink, tek their shirts off to tan their pasty bodies in the sun. It's what me dad used to do. Starts off fun then gets nasty. Mark my words: they'll be fighting later.

Dev   You ever hear from him?

Chris   Who?

Dev   Your dad.

Chris   He passed.

Dev   When?

Chris   Few months back.

Dev   Why didn't you tell me?

Beat.

Chris   How's yer mum?

Dev   Ok.

Chris   Still in that place?

Dev   Yeah. She didn't like it at first, but there are cinema rooms, activities, away days . . .

Chris   Does she do any of them?

Dev   No, but it's better than sitting alone. Expensive though.

Chris   You get what you pay for.

Dev   My point exactly.

Chris   This is a deluxe room now, pal.

Dev   What's deluxe about it?

Chris *has no answer.*

Dev   I'm sorry about your dad.

Chris *sips the drink.*

Chris   Rula Lenska was a redhead and the orange made the drink look red.

Dev   You sure?

Chris No . . . but we had a few of these and then we hit the beach in Portinatx, where we pulled those birds from Doncaster.

Dev Yes!

Chris Mine had a neck brace, which was a bit weird.

Dev I remember.

Chris Those were the days.

Dev Yeah . . . but I wasn't like you two.

Chris In what way?

Dev Confident with women.

Chris You were alright.

Dev I was always left holding the pints. Never knew the rules.

Chris Who does?

Dev Michael did.

Chris You done alright.

Dev I've felt single most of my life.

Chris Mebbe you don't want to be in a relationship?

Dev No, I just can't tolerate it, but I can no longer tolerate being alone.

Chris The psychotherapy has helped then?

Dev One tries. What about you?

Chris What about me?

Dev Is your life sorted?

Chris My life is sweet, pal.

Dev So, why are you ogling twenty-three-year-olds out of a balcony window like a dirty old man?

A silence.

Chris   I'm not an old man.

Dev   You're fifty.

Chris   Forty-nine.

Dev   For the next six days . . .

A silence.

Chris   What good's it done you, eh? Talking? You're still
the same person I met at eighteen, minus several thousand
quid, but that's cool if that's what you wanna do. But it's not
my thing, and if I wish to appreciate the beauty of a girl who
is twenty-eight or twenty-one for that matter from a balcony
window or from anywhere else, within reason, that's my
choice. I don't need your questions and I don't need your
analysis.

Dev   Sorry . . . I didn't mean /

Chris *silences him with a chord on the guitar.*

The song is improvised in the style of a Guns N' Roses ballad.

Chris (*sings*)
　　Don't need questions
　　Don't need analysis
　　Leads to nowhere
　　Leads to paralysis
　　I just want to go away
　　On a sunny holiday
　　Wishing all my cares away
　　Under a blue sky
　　Under a blue sky

At some point during the above **Dev** *starts drumming on his suitcase
and takes over lead vocals while* **Chris** *keeps playing underneath
and does backing vocals.*

Dev (*sings*)
　　I took pills
　　Now I'm on dialysis
　　My kidneys failed

So, I'm using Alice's
She doesn't need them anyway
Cos she's sadly passed away
Shouldn't have tried to overtake
On the inside
On the inside

Chris/Dev (*singing*)
Under a blue sky
On the inside
Under a blue blue sky
On the in-in-side
On the inside of the blue blue sky

Chris (*stops playing*)   What's the hook, 'blue sky' or 'inside'?

Dev   Both? 'On the inside of the blue sky.'

Chris *tries out the riff. He starts developing it into a new tune. He stops.*

Chris   We wrote good songs – me and you.

Dev   Perhaps 'I was too close to the work'.

Beat.

Chris's *phone pings.*

Dev   Is that our lead singer?

Chris (*reading message*)   Yeah.

Dev   What's he saying?

Chris   He's not going to make it out today.

Dev   Of course.

Chris   But he sent us this.

Chris *shows* **Dev** *his phone.*

Dev   Jesus! Is that a donkey's . . .?

Chris   Aye.

Dev   The man has daughters.

Chris   They're the worst.

Dev   I do wonder sometimes . . . how he has kids and I don't.

Chris   Ask yer therapist.

Dev   I do.

Chris   If you had kids you wouldn't be here now.

Dev   I'd be strolling down the beach with her hand in hand.

Chris   Chasing her down the beach more like, her screaming: 'I hate you, you twat!'

Dev   You know, when people ask about it, I never know what to say. I can be having a perfectly decent time, then someone will ask and everything changes. I was at conference last month and this author – manly type – says to me in the pub, 'So, are you a family man, Dev?' and I said . . . yes. Made up this story about having two kids – Derek and Marina.

Chris   Yer what?

Dev   Said I was separated from their mother, who lived in Brighton.

Chris   You named your children Derek and Marina?

Dev   They're not real.

Chris   Who names a baby Derek?

Dev   Do you never get caught out like that?

Chris   No.

Dev   Never think about it?

Chris   No. Anyway it's not too late.

Dev   Isn't it?

Chris   Men can have 'em at seventy.

Dev   Possibly, but you'd be old when they're ten. They'd spend their twenties wiping your arse.

Chris   Want a drink before you jump off balcony?

His phone pings again. He looks at it and grins.

Dev   What's she doing with the donkey now?

Chris   Nah . . . it's this bird from choir. She's into BDSM. Sends me photos of her tied up and shit.

Dev   Who takes them?

Chris   What?

Dev   If she's tied up who takes the photos?

Chris   Dunno.

*He shows **Dev** his phone.*

Dev   She has a kind face.

Chris   Sometimes you worry me.

Dev   Says the man whose girlfriend's tied to a tree.

Chris   She's not my girlfriend.

Dev   Ok.

Chris   First date was odd, to be fair. She invites me to Epping Forest and she's strung up to a tree and she wants me to whip her, like really whip her, and I'm only in it for a shag, so I have to kinda pretend, 'Take that, you dirty bitch! Take that!'. But actually I'm trying not to hurt her, but she likes being hurt, like whipped and shit, like wounds, and I actually find it quite distressing, not to mention the stress on the fingers having to undo all those knots after. Honestly, *that was* agony. But in the end I got into it, not whipping her, just the whole theatre of it.

Dev   Did you never try Guardian Soulmates?

Chris   She's an interesting person. She's into picking wild mushrooms.

Dev   Well, if you're in the forest . . .

Chris   Makes amazing stews.

Dev   I had about four thousand dates on Guardian Soulmates.

Chris   See, you do get action.

Dev   No, just drank lots of coffee.

Chris's *phone pings again. He clocks it, starts to text.*

Chris   Let's go Pacha, do a pill.

Dev   Tonight?

Chris   You're not going to be boring, are you?

Dev   No, but tonight I just want to chill.

Chris *drinks his drink.*

Dev   Tomorrow definitely . . . There's a museum looks interesting – Museum of the Marionette.

Chris *looks at* **Dev** *and slowly downs his drink.*

Beat.

From below there's the smash of glass and raised voices.

Chris   What did I tell you?

He looks to see what's going on.

Look at them with their tats and their Burberry hats – just embarrassing.

He starts to get ready.

Dev   You off to Pacha then?

Chris   Dunno.

Dev   I'll definitely come out tomorrow.

Chris *goes into his bag and pulls out some cologne.*

Dev *sits on the bed with his book.*

Dev   Want to finish this.

Chris   What is it?

Dev   'Death in Venice'.

Chris   Saw the film of that once. Not right. And very slow.

Chris *sprays the cologne in the air and dances into it.* **Dev** *wafts it away jokily with his book.*

Chris   Tom Ford. Three hundred quid this.

Dev   And you won't spend fifty on a direct flight?

Chris   It's got oud in it.

Dev   What's oud?

Chris   It's like this aromatic stuff. Ultra-masculine.

Dev   It's pronounced wood.

Chris   Got that too, pal!

He shapes his hair in the mirror with his hands.

He tucks his shacket into his shorts.

Chris   Will you be okay on your own, dear?

Dev   Yes, Mum. I've got my book.

He checks out the tucked-in shacket – he pulls his stomach in, then thinks better of it and pulls the shacket out before finally spraying some Tom Ford down his shorts. He ties a hoodie round his waist, then takes it off and throws it round his shoulders.

Dev   Don't take the hoodie.

Chris   Gets nippy at night.

Dev *shakes his head.* **Chris** *takes the hoodie off.*

Chris   Right then. Wish me luck.

Dev   Smelling of oud, mate, you hardly need it.

Chris *goes.*

Alone, **Dev** *sits on the bed for a few seconds surveying the room and the wardrobe. He starts to read his book.*

Maybe Mahler's Theme to the Death In Venice *film plays into:*

Scene Two

Night. The same.

The room in semi-darkness. The wardrobe door is ajar revealing a depth of murk. A line of pillows and other objects have been placed down the middle of the bed to demarcate Dev's half. A light dances round the edge of the closed shutters. Somewhere there is the crying of a child. It stops.

The sound of a key in the door. **Holly** *and* **Chris** *enter, whispering.*

Holly   Why's he gone to bed?

Chris   He's got a bad back.

Holly   I'm good with backs.

Chris   You go onto the balcony. I'll make the drinks.

Holly   I just wanna have a look at him.

Chris   No, you'll wake him.

Holly   Just a little look.

Holly *peers at* **Dev**.

Holly   Aw, he's sleeping.

Chris   Yes, he's sleeping, go onto the balcony.

Holly   Alright!

Chris *goes into the bathroom.* **Holly** *sees the guitar, starts lightly strumming.* **Chris** *emerges from the bathroom.*

Chris   What are you doing?

Holly   I found this – a child's guitar.

Chris   It's not a child's guitar, it's a travel guitar.

Holly   What's a travel guitar?

Chris   It's a special guitar for . . . doesn't matter. Take it outside and don't play it.

Holly *goes onto the balcony. Sound of guitar.* **Chris** *goes to the bathroom to make drinks. As he is emerging,* **Holly** *comes back in.*

Chris   What now?

Holly   It was lonely on balcony.

Chris *hands her a drink.*

Chris   Have this. You'll like it.

Holly   What is it?

Chris   A Rula Lenska.

Holly *takes a sip.*

Holly   Did you piss in this?

Chris   No. Keep sipping, it will grow on you.

They exit to balcony. Sound of guitar and giggling.

Chris *re-enters.*

Chris   Wait there. I've got some crisps.

Chris *starts hunting for crisps.* **Holly** *comes in.*

Holly   Where are you?

Chris   I'm looking for the crisps.

Holly   I'll help.

Chris *and* **Holly** *search for the crisps, looking in and around the bed where* **Dev** *is sleeping. At some point,* **Holly** *looks under the sheet.*

Chris   Don't do that.

Holly   He might have had the munchies.

They continue searching. At some point, **Holly** *clambers over* **Dev**.

Holly   Have you not found them yet? I'm starving.

Dev   They're in the wardrobe.

Holly   He's awake!

Chris   Go back to sleep, mate.

Dev   I'm awake now.

Holly   Sorry. We were looking for crisps.

Dev   I heard.

Holly   You've got a bad back.

Dev   It's fine.

Holly   I'm good with backs. Left or right?

Dev   Left, but it's fine.

Holly   Lie on the floor.

Dev   What?

Holly   Come on.

Dev   I'm ok.

Holly (*turns the light on*)   Come on, I know about these things. I'm a dancer.

Dev (*clocking her*)   Ok . . . let's do this.

Dev *gets himself onto the floor on his front.*

Holly   No, roll over! Knees to chest.

Dev   Shouldn't we have a drink first?

Holly   Pull yer stomach muscles in and try and get yer back flat on the floor . . .

Dev *brings his knees up to his chest.*

Holly   When I press down, you breathe out, ok?

Dev   I'm Dev, by the way.

Holly *puts some of her body weight on* **Dev***'s knees.*

They repeat. **Dev** *sighs out painfully. He is unexpectedly crying.*

Holly   What's up?

Dev   I don't know.

Holly *puts a tender hand on* **Dev***'s shoulder.*

Chris *has clocked this.*

Holly (*to* **Chris**)   Where are these crisps, you?

Chris   What kind of dancer are you?

Holly   A good one.

Dev   I mean contemporary? Ballet?

Holly   Both.

Dev   Where did you train?

Holly   Miss Ella's Ballet School. And Danny's Dice Bar.

Chris   Receta Campesina or Sabor Jamón?

Holly   Both.

Chris *throws the packets to* **Holly**.

Holly   So, you two bessies?

Chris   Pals, yeah.

Holly   Sharing a bed, eh?

Chris   No, you can push these apart.

Dev   That's what he says.

Holly   I don't mind . . .

Chris *We're not.*

Holly *laughs.*

Dev He's not my type anyway.

Holly My pal's pissed off.

Chris Why?

Holly Cos she's boring.

Chris Who is your pal?

Holly Amy. You met her downstairs.

Chris Did I?

Holly Dark hair, sat next to me when you joined.

Dev Girls' holiday?

Holly Yeah. We love a bit of Pantinos. Been coming here years. What 'bout you?

Dev We were here last century.

Chris We came here on holiday when we were at uni, stayed in this very room.

Holly Really?

Dev Chris thought it'd be fun to return for his big birthday.

Holly Happy birthday!

Chris It's not till Friday.

Holly How old?

Chris Age is just a number.

Dev Sixty.

Chris No!

Holly Friday's best day round here cos it's Robbie's karaoke.

Dev Lovely!

Holly He makes it fun, does Robbie. Gets everyone to dress up as eighties pop stars.

Dev Who are you going as?

Holly (*sings in an exaggerated way*)
  I decided long ago
  That I would go as /

Dev (*sings*) Kylie Minogue.

Holly *laughs.*

Chris Sadly, we won't be here Friday.

Holly Why not?

Chris Our friend'll be out by then and he's taking us somewhere else.

Holly Well, you'll miss a great night.

Chris You've got a great voice by the way.

Holly Give over.

Chris Rock 'n' roll voice that . . .

Holly If you think mine's good, you should hear Amy. She was professional.

Chris Mebbe we can have a sing-song?

Holly Mebbe we can.

Chris (*sidling up to* **Holly** *faux seductively*) Mebbe if I show you my singing, you can show me yer dancing.

Holly *responds with a rapid dance move towards* **Dev** *– at once sexy, but also athletic, owning the sensuality it contains – a kind of physical dare.*

Dev's *fizzy water explodes all over himself.*

Dev Sorry. Sorry.

Chris   What you doing?

Dev   I love your tattoos.

Holly   Ta. You got any?

Dev   Not great on my skin tone.

Holly   Not true . . . you should get one. Put it on yer Insta for yer fans.

Dev   My fans?

Holly   You're a pop star, aren't ya? He said you were in a band.

Dev   Thirty years ago.

Chris   We started off in one, but then we split.

Holly   What were you called?

Chris   The Frampton Sound Experiment.

Holly   Were you any good?

Chris   We were banging. We pressed our own single, became John Peel's 'Band of the Week'.

Holly   Who?

Dev   He played it once.

Chris   Got interest from Q Prime off the back of it.

Holly   Who?

Chris   Peter Mensch, Cliff Bernstein . . . manage Metallica, Def Leppard, Chili Peppers.

Holly   Oh right.

Dev   Alas, it didn't work out.

Holly   Why not?

Chris   He left.

Dev   I got a scholarship to study abroad – big opportunity – couldn't turn it down.

Holly   What do you do now?

Dev   I teach at university.

Holly   Teach what?

Dev   Music.

Chris   Those who can't . . .

Dev   Thank you.

Chris   You've either got it or you haven't and if you've got it you'll stick at it.

Holly   Have you got it?

Chris   Bucketloads.

Holly (*to* **Dev**)   So, what is it you teach yer students?

Dev   We look at a range of things . . . music in the community, music therapy, music management, as well as music performance of course.

Chris   You should hear some of it.

Dev   It's not to Chris's taste.

Chris   They play it to enemy solders to induce confessions.

Dev   Chris likes simple songs for simple people.

Chris   Better than someone having a fit while blowing into a flugel horn.

Dev   I love all music, pop, world music, classical . . . I recently wrote a book on Dvořák.

Holly   Who's that?

Dev   A composer . . . wrote a lot of famous tunes. Some you'll know very well.

Holly   You wrote an actual book?

Dev   I've written three.

Chris *grabs his guitar and strums a chord.*

Chris (*sings and plays à la George Formby*)
    Ooh there's nothing steamier
    Than a life in academia
    Lectures and vivas
    Make you feel alive

    Anticipation
    Reading your dissertation
    Stick my hand in yer essay
    And let's hope things get mess-ay

    Wanna see me at full size?
    Stay up all night and revise
    Coz I can't get a lob-on
    For less than a 2:1

    If you're shaved or if you're hairy
    Take me to the li-brary
    Peer review me till it hurts
    Lecture me until I squirt

    But a final word of warning:
    When you wake up in the morning
    (*The song dissolves into speech now.*)
    It'll hit you that you've shagged a fucking lecturer whose
    life revolves round books and people who theorise for a
    living cos the real world's too scary for them.

An awkward beat.

Holly *claps enthusiastically.*

Chris   Bit of fun.

Holly   I'll get Amy down here! (*Grabs phone.*) Oh it's fucked
cos I dropped it in the pool.

Chris (*indicating hotel phone*)   Use ours.

Holly (*on hotel phone*)   Amy! Amy! What you doing? . . .Well, get yerself down 'ere . . . we're in . . .

Chris   547.

Holly   Room 547 – we're having a party . . . No, it's not them. It's two old guys. They've got a guitar and we're having a sing-song – you'll love it . . . Put yer face back on and come down. Come on . . . You'll love it. Please.

She puts the phone down disappointed.

Silence.

Chris   We're here all week.

Holly   I'm going for a waz.

She goes to the bathroom.

Beat.

Dev (*lowering voice*)   Well, she's . . .

Chris   What?

Dev   I wouldn't say no.

Chris   To what?

Dev   What do you think?

Chris *scoffs.*

Dev   You were the one saying I needed to get laid.

Chris   Evidently you do, mate.

Dev   What's that supposed to mean?

Chris   Throwing yourself at her?

Dev   I think she's into me actually.

Chris   Do ya?

Dev   Where did you meet her anyway?

Chris   By the pool.

Dev   I thought you found those people embarrassing.

Chris   I thought you despised them . . . I thought you were impotent.

Dev   Sorry?

Chris   You've retired from sex and material whatsits.

Dev   That doesn't mean I'm impotent.

Chris   Well, I saw her first.

Dev   What are we, teenagers?

Chris   Mebbe . . . cos I were snogging the face off her out there.

Dev   Course you were – that's why she got into bed with me.

Chris   She was looking for crisps.

Dev   So your sexual overtures . . . made her hungry for a salty snack?

Chris   Are you from the 1950s?

Dev   This is pathetic.

Chris   I'll tell you what's pathetic, mate – you playing the sympathy card. Ooooh, my back! Ooooh, I'm crying!

Dev   Better than playing the musician card. Been pulling that one for thirty years.

Chris   Pulling what?

Dev   You're a TEFL teacher, mate. You're not Julio Iglesias.

Chris   Uncalled for.

Dev   Your song was uncalled for. You'd worked on those lyrics.

Chris   As if I could be bothered?

Dev   You and Michael always made me the whipping boy.

Beat.

Chris   Look . . . if you think you've got a chance, go for it.

Dev   You saw her first.

Chris   Fuck it.

Dev   I'm sorry for what I said about Julio Iglesias.

Holly *comes out of the toilet. She is holding something behind her back.*

Holly (*to* **Chris**)   Oi! I got a bone to pick with you.

Chris   What?

Holly   You said you only had that whisky and tonic – what's this?

From behind her back she brandishes a bottle of tequila.

Chris   I was saving it.

Holly   What for?

Chris   My birthday, for when our mate comes.

Holly   Can we open it?

Chris   I'm saving it.

Dev   Do you honestly think Michael's going to turn up here with Dave Drexler?

Chris *wants to say yes.*

Holly   Tequila makes me wild.

Chris   Mebbe we shouldn't then, for the sake of the furniture.

Holly   We're on holiday.

Chris   Go on then.

Holly   Shots! Shots! Shots! Shots! Shots! Shots! Shots! Shots!

Holly *dances as she opens the tequila. She's wild.*

Dev *beams at her.*

There is a knock at the door.

Chris   That'll be next door telling us to keep it down.

Holly *keeps dancing.*

Another knock at the door.

Chris *answers the door to a dark-haired woman, mid-forties, wearing jeans, blouse, not glammed up. This is* **Amy**, *who speaks from the doorway.*

Amy (*seeing* **Holly**)   Holly, luv! Holly!

Holly (*overjoyed*)   Amy! You made it! This is her! This is Amy!

Amy   Hiya!

(*To* **Holly**.) It's Darren, luv.

Holly   What does he want?

Amy   He can't get Ryan down. He's been trying for hours. Trying your phone too.

Holly   I dropped it in pool.

Amy   Darren's got an interview in the morning and they can't find Mr Snakey.

Holly   Fuck's sake.

Amy   You know how Ryan gets when he can't find Mr Snakey.

Holly   Give it here.

She grabs the phone from **Amy** *and takes it out onto the balcony.*

Holly (*off*)   What's going on? . . . I thought I told you not to fucking ring me unless it's an emergency . . .

Beat.

Amy   Sorry to interrupt.

Chris   No.

Dev   Come in.

Amy   I won't.

Dev   We're just cracking open the tequila.

Amy   I were reading in bed.

Dev   Me too.

Amy   What you got?

Dev   'Death in Venice'.

Amy   A whodunnit?

Dev   No.

Chris   Nearly is.

Amy   What's it about?

Dev   Hard to explain.

Chris   It's about a writer on holiday in Venice, clocks a fourteen-year-old lad, follows him round.

Amy   What for?

Chris   Why do you think?

Dev   It's an exploration of humanity's impossible desire for eternity as expressed in youth.

Amy   Does he manage it?

Dev   No.

Amy   What happens?

Dev   He dies on the beach.

Amy   Who?

Dev   The writer.

Chris   Wanks himself to death.

Dev   What are you reading?

Amy   'The Rochdale Murders' – about five unsolved murders in Rochdale between 1981 and 1993.

Dev   Sounds gory.

Amy   It is, but I find it relaxing.

Holly (*off*)   'Kin hell, Darren, sort it out!

Amy   So, which one of you's the singer?

Chris   I am.

Amy   Where do you do that?

Chris   All over.

Dev   She said you're a singer, too?

Amy   I used to be. Just weddings and parties in Hull mainly and surrounds.

Chris   Perhaps I heard you.

Amy   You from Hull?

Chris   Born and bred, but I live in London now.

Amy   That's funny.

Chris   Tell you what, stay for a drink, and give us a song.

Amy   No, but if you play one, mebbe I will stay for a little bit.

Holly (*coming in from off*)   I'll be home soon. Now be good and go to sleep. Mr Snakey will look after you till I am back. He will. He's good is Mr Snakey. You know he is.

Right! Shots!

Dev   All good . . .?

Holly   Yeah. You got any glasses?

Chris   In the bathroom.

Holly *goes into the bathroom to find glasses.*

Beat.

Dev   So . . . Mr Snakey . . .

Amy   It's her son's cuddly toy – he won't sleep without it.

Dev   Oh.

Amy   Ryan. He's five – heart of gold, but terrible abandonment issues . . .

Dev   Oh.

Amy   Usually his sister Rianne's there to help, but she's on a school trip at the moment.

Dev   How old's she?

Amy   Ten.

Dev   And Darren is . . .?

Amy   Her ex. Ryan's dad – bit useless, but does his best.

Holly *comes out of the toilet with glasses.*

Holly   Let's play 'Truth or Dare'.

Amy   No, luv.

Holly   While we got the shots poured. You fellas are up for it?

Chris   Why not?

Holly   Rules are I ask the questions and either you answer and we move on, or if you don't want to answer you have to drink and I give you a dare to do.

Chris   Are those the actual rules?

Holly   They are now.

Amy   I don't want to play this, luv.

Holly   Don't be boring. (*To* **Dev**.) You, you're up for it?

Dev   Sure am.

Holly   Right, first question (*To* **Chris**.) – to you. Have you ever . . . had sex in a graveyard?

Chris   Yes.

Holly   Ok . . . to Amy – have you . . . ever . . . had sex on public transport?

Amy   No, luv.

Holly   If you just answer it'll get boring.

Amy   It is boring.

Dev   Let's think of better questions then.

Holly   Exactly! Ok. (*To* **Dev**.) You. Have you ever got in trouble with a student . . .

Dev *hesitates.*

Dev   No.

Holly   You hesitated.

Dev   Did I?

Chris   Well, have you or haven't ya?

Dev *drinks.*

Chris   Dirty bastard.

Dev   No.

Holly   Right, your dare is . . .

Chris   Hang on. You kept that quiet. What did you do?

Dev   I didn't *do* anything. I went through a phase of cycling in. Kept some spare clothes in the office, and one day I was running late, forgot to lock the door, and the students arrived early.

Chris   So they saw you naked?

Dev   No, I had my pants on. And a shirt. But one of them felt traumatized and reported me to the Dean. I had to sit in isolation in the office while they carried out a formal investigation, which was mortifying, but thankfully the whole thing blew over.

Chris   And this, my friends, is how it starts . . .

Holly   Right, your dare is jump in the pool naked.

Dev   No.

Holly   You have to.

Dev   There are balconies all round with families – I'll get lynched.

Holly   Don't matter.

Dev   Besides I just explained the whole story so . . .

Holly   No, you drank. You chose to drink so you have to do the dare.

Chris   She's got a point.

Dev   I'm not jumping in the pool naked.

Holly   It's the rules.

Dev   I will do a dare – just not that one.

Holly   Ok . . . jump in the sea naked.

Dev   At this time of night?

Chris   You just said you would.

Holly   Fuck's sake, I'll go in with ya if ya like . . .

Dev   That I will do.

Chris   That's not a dare. You can't just choose your dare.

Dev   She's the rule master, so keep your fucking nose out of it.

Chris   Fuck this.

Amy   Boys! Don't fight.

Chris   It's the rules of the game.

Amy   It's a silly game.

Holly   A toast: to Ibiza, to Hotel Pantinos, to holiday flings and sex on the beach!

Dev (*a little too loudly*)   Yes!

Everyone looks at him.

Amy   We should really have salt and lemon with this.

Dev *downs the tequila.*

Dev (*to* **Holly**)   Shall we?

Chris   Now he's keen.

Dev   I reckon it'll be good for my back.

Chris   It's not meant to be good for your back.

Holly   Why don't you come – we'll all swim naked?

Chris   Nah, you're alright.

Holly   Ok, stay here, and play her yer song.

Dev (*to* **Holly**)   Are we swimming?

Holly   Come on. No breast stroke.

Dev *laughs slightly nervously.*

Amy   Careful!

Dev   I'm a gentleman.

Amy   It was you I was talking to. She's trouble.

Holly   I'll be good, promise. You two: (*Suggestively.*) Behave yerselves!

Dev *and* **Holly** *leave.*

A long silence.

Amy   Did you not want to go with them?

Chris   No.

Amy   You can if you want.

Chris   I don't.

He is in a sulk.

Amy   Are you gonna play me this song?

Chris   Not right now.

Beat.

So how did you get into it all . . . music?

Amy   School choir. What about you?

Chris   Me dad was a session drummer in the sixties and seventies.

Amy   Who with?

Chris   Loads. The Small Faces, The Animals. He played on 'The House of the Rising Sun'.

Amy   You're kidding?

Chris   No.

Amy   I used to love singing that one. (*Beat.*) Does he still play?

Chris   He's dead.

Amy   Sorry.

Chris   Don't be. He was never there.

Amy   It's not easy being a parent.

Chris   I wouldn't know.

Amy   Neither would I to be fair.

Chris   No kids?

Amy   Old, free and single.

Chris   You're not old.

Amy   I am . . . and invisible.

Chris   You're not invisible either.

Amy   You didn't remember me from downstairs.

Chris   Cos I was talking to yer mate.

Amy   Fellas are always doing that.

Chris   To be honest, I know she's your friend and that, but I find her a bit much.

Amy   She is.

Without meaning to, **Chris** *has started strumming 'The House of the Rising Sun'.* **Amy** *sings the first verse.*

Chris (*stops playing*)   Your voice . . . it's soulful.

Amy   Bet you say that to all the girls.

Chris   Did you gig a lot round Hull?

Amy   Aye, back in the day.

Chris   What were you called?

Amy   Peppermint Twist.

Chris *laughs.*

Amy   Shit name – I know.

Chris   I saw yer.

Amy   You did not.

Chris   Would have been at the Adelphi in the nineties . . . I used to work on the door every third Friday of the month. Do you remember?

Amy   No . . . were we shit?

Chris   The band was . . . but you . . . far from it.

They laugh.

It was you and that biker fella you were with.

Amy   Mark . . . on bass . . . Jason on lead and Horny John on drums.

Chris   Why was he called Horny John?

Amy   Not cos he played the horn.

They laugh again.

Chris   I think I bought you a drink that night, do ya remember?

Amy   Sorry.

They laugh again.

A long silence.

Neither of them move.

Chris   Nightcap?

Amy   Go on.

Chris *pours himself and* **Amy** *a drink. They down it.*

Amy   Didn't expect that.

Chris   Me neither.

Some drunken voices, laughter coming down the corridor.

A long beat as the voices pass, the laughter subsides.

Amy   What's that lovely smell?

Chris   It's Tom Ford . . It's got oud in it.

Amy   What's that?

Chris   Don't matter.

He picks up the guitar and strums the chords for 'The House of the Rising Sun'. They sing the last two verses together.

Fade out.

Act Two

Scene One

Six days later.

For a minute we are transported into the heart of the Ibiza clubbing scene – a dance floor, laser lights, strobes, DJ on decks, pumping techno, revellers lost in a riff, losing their minds.

This segues into karaoke night at the Hotel Pantinos. Holly, as Whitney, singing 'I Will Always Love You'.

9 p.m. The karaoke continues downstairs.

The room more lived in. The suitcase put away. Three bottles of cava – one open – on the table and a half-eaten birthday cake.

Amy, *in a slinky black dress, hair tied back, is eating the cake. She has stepped out of her stilettos and hung her leather jacket on a chair.*

Chris *enters red-faced from the sun – hair/wig puffed up in a kind of bouffant.*

Both are tipsy. The attraction between them is palpable.

Chris   You eating my cake?

Amy   Want some?

Chris   Yeah.

He puts his arm round her waist. She squashes some cake into his face. They play-fight with the cake – she squeals. He kisses her neck.

Chris   I always fancied that Belinda Carlisle . . .

Amy   I had a thing for that Rod Stewart.

Chris   Yeah?

Amy   Yeah.

Chris   Well, not that it matters, but I'm supposed to be Jon Bon Jovi.

Beat.

Chris   I need a waz.

He goes into the bathroom. She sits on the bed.

Chris (*off*)   Do I look like Rod Stewart?

Amy   It's the red face, luv – need some aftersun on that.

Chris   Nah, in my opinion the whole sun cream industry needs a government shake-up.

Amy   Write to your MP.

Chris *laughs.*

Amy   When's your flight tomorrow?

Chris   Afternoon. You?

Amy   Late. I were thinking of tekking one of them boat trips round the caves in the morning . . . but then I thought . . .

Chris   What?

Amy   Dunno . . . thought we might tek a last walk along the beach, say goodbye . . .

Beat.

. . . we don't have to . . .

Chris   No, I'd like to . . . And when I'm home, I'll bell ya, we can grab a drink at the Polar Bear.

Amy *smiles. She takes her hair down and sits on the bed.*

Chris *appears at the door of the bathroom in only his tight underpants which have some kind of Spanish cartoon on them.*

Amy   Christ!

Chris   Sorry, they only had kids' left in the Mini Mart.

Beat.

They laugh. He sits on the bed.

Amy   What if they come in?

Chris   They won't.

Amy   How do you know?

Chris   We have a code, Dev and I, if one of us . . . you know
. . . needs the room.

Amy   What is it?

Chris   Off to Portinatx – do not disturb. Little in-joke from
when we were here before.

Amy   So, am I just your latest conquest?

Chris   No. No.

Amy   You fellas are always mad for it till you get it, then
you're gone.

Chris   I'm still here.

Amy   For now.

Chris   Who left you?

Amy   They all did. Some to their mams, some to their exes,
some to their jobs, some to their tiny fascinations . . .

Chris   What about your biker guy?

Amy   Mark?

Chris   Where'd he go?

Amy   Off down the M62 on his Kawasaki.

Chris   Rotter.

Amy   No, he was a knobhead, not a rotter.

Chris   What's the difference?

Amy   A rotter breaks yer heart on purpose. A knobhead
doesn't mean to.

She seems a little distant.

Chris   You ok?

Amy   Tell me about you . . .

Chris   What?

Amy   About yer big love . . . the one that got away?

Chris   Laura Grogan. Kiss chase. 1982. Almost caught her, but then she slipped out of her cardy, got away.

Amy   Or were you the one always running away?

Chris *smiles.*

Amy   Do you want to run now?

Chris   A bit.

Amy   Why?

Chris   Cos it's a bit weird doing therapy in these underpants.

She laughs.

Chris   A bit of me always runs.

Amy   Like your dad?

Beat.

Chris   I went to see him the night he died, for 'closure' . . . He had nothing for me, no wisdom, just kept pulling at his clothes, his hair. At one point he did open his eyes and speak . . .

Amy   What did he say?

Chris   Make sure you service the boiler. Delirious I guess. Unless he really did want me to service it.

She laughs.

Point is we don't work it out. We can talk about it, make ourselves feel better for a bit, but we are who we are.

Amy   Do you miss him?

Beat.

Chris   Me dad? (*Beat.*) Didn't really know him to be honest.

He stands.

Amy   Where you going?

Chris   I find misery a turn-off.

Amy   I find honesty a turn-on . . . emotional nakedness.

Chris   What about real nakedness?

Amy   Not so much, but in your case it's alright.

Chris *sits.*

Beat.

Chris (*sincere, emotional*)   I think you're lovely, you know. A goddess – any man would be lucky to have you.

Amy   Where did that come from?

Beat.

What do you want for yer birthday . . .?

Chris   You already got me the cake . . . (*Off her look.*) Oh! You mean . . .? Oh . . . You decide.

Amy   Shall I tie you up?

Chris   What with?

Amy *reaches over and grabs an iPhone cable.*

Chris   That's Dev's.

Amy   He won't mind.

Chris   He will.

Amy   Don't tell him then. Come on.

Chris *lies on the bed while she ties one of his hands to the bedstead.*

Chris   It'll never hold – not enough friction.

*Amy successfully binds **Chris**'s hand to the bedstead. With his free hand, he tries to unzips her dress.*

Amy   What else we got?

She gets the cable from the other side.

Chris   Mine's the one metre, won't be long enough.

Amy successfully binds his other hand using his cable and looks to him for a response.

Chris   Are you good at DIY?

Amy   Happy birthday!

She kisses him tenderly.

Suddenly there is a noise at the door.

Dev *and* **Holly**'s *voices.*

Dev (*off*)   He wouldn't have had my songs.

Holly (*off*)   He's got over forty thousand.

Chris   He hasn't got a key.

A key in the door. The door unlocks.

Amy *pulling up her dress.*

Chris   What you doing? Save me!

Amy   Save yourself.

She scarpers into the bathroom.

Dev (*as Stevie Wonder*) *appears in the doorway with* **Holly** (*as Whitney*) *behind.*

Dev   Look, I'm not a karaoke guy.

Chris   Dev! Dev! I'm in here.

Dev   What are you doing?

Chris   What does it look like?

Beat.

Did I not tell you we were going to be using the room?

Dev   Did you?

Chris   Did I not say, 'I'm off to Portinatx. Do not disturb.'

Dev   I thought you said, 'I'm off to the jacks, too much reverb.'

Chris   What?

Dev   On the karaoke machine.

Chris   Why would I go to the jacks if there was too much reverb?

Dev   To get away from it?

Holly   Hiya, Chris.

Chris   Hello.

Holly   Bit tied up?

Chris   Yeah, ha ha. (*To* **Dev**.) How do you even have a key?

Dev   I got a spare from reception. I thought it would be useful.

Holly   Where's Amy?

Chris   Bathroom.

Holly   Have you seen my lippy? It's in a little red purse.

Chris   No

Holly (*entering*)   I'll just have a little look. Must be here somewhere.

She hunts for the purse.

Did you enjoy the karaoke?

Chris   Yes.

Holly   It's fun in't it? Bit of glamour. I love a bit of glamour. I could have been a pop star I reckon. And people go to a lot of trouble. D'ya see fella came as Bananarama – all three in one? Bit of mess to be fair. No, keep it simple I reckon – Stevie, Whitney, Rod Stewart . . .

Chris   Bon Jovi.

Holly   What?

Chris   Look, can you just give us a minute?

Holly   Oh yeah. Found it anyway.

Holly *takes a little bag of Mandy out of the purse and dabs it on her tongue. Then, seeing herself in the mirror, she starts to puff up her hair.*

Chris   Like, now?

Holly   Oh, yeah. Dev!

Dev   What?

Holly   Let's give him a minute.

Dev   Sure . . . (*Beat.*) Is that my iPhone charger?

Chris   Yes.

Dev   That was from the Apple Store.

Chris   Can you just fuck off?

Holly   Come on, you perv.

Dev *and* **Holly** *retreat.*

Chris *struggles to free himself.*

Amy *comes out of the bathroom and unties* **Chris**. *Though flustered, they are laughing. He might call her a 'Judas'.* **Chris** *goes into the bathroom to get changed.*

Holly (*off*)   Right, we're coming back in in 5, 4, 3, 2, 1.

Holly *and* **Dev** *come in,* **Holly** *struggling to contain her amusement.*

Amy   Shut it!

Holly   I didn't say anything . . . though I didn't know you were into kinky sex.

Amy   I'm on holiday. How's the karaoke?

Holly   Fab, except Stevie Wonder here wouldn't sing.

Dev   It's not my bag.

Holly   You just have to drink and let it out.

Dev   Sometimes I prefer to keep it in.

Holly   That's *why* you drink.

Dev   And I wasn't that comfortable with the DJ blacked up as Tina Turner.

Holly   He don't mean nothing by it.

Dev   It's a bit offensive.

Holly   I weren't offended.

Dev   Maybe you should be.

Holly   And mebbe you shouldn't tell me what to think.

Dev   I just think /

Holly   D'ya ever not think? D'ya ever just do something cos you feel like it? Mebbe it's stupid, mebbe it's funny, but you just do it and see what happens?

Amy   He's got a point, luv, it was a bit tasteless.

Holly   It was a fun night. We're having fun!

Chris *comes out of the bathroom.*

Chris   Right! Who wants a drink, we got cava or cava . . . or whisky and tonic.

Dev/Holly/Amy   Cava.

Chris (*to* **Holly**)   I liked your Whitney.

Holly   Didn't get to do my favourite.

Amy   Yet.

They sing and dance to the first two lines of the chorus from 'I Wanna Dance with Somebody' by Whitney Houston.

Chris   Well, the night is young.

Dev (*pointed*)   Like stepping back in time.

Amy   Dev's a bit offended with the DJ's costume.

Chris   I thought it was quite funny, the way he kept saying: 'I'm simply the best'.

Dev   Hilarious.

Chris   Chill out, mate.

Dev   There's a weight of history to these things, to blackface, to certain words . . .

Chris   Says Stevie Wonder!

Dev   That's different.

Chris   If he'd whited up I wouldn't have cared.

Dev   He was white.

Chris   Call me Honky any time.

Dev   It's not the same. In order to be similar, I'd have to add something more personal to the insult.

Chris   Like what?

Dev   Desperate man child Honky . . .

Chris   I'm ok with that.

Dev   . . . self-deluding, middle-aged, scrawny, pathetic, fatherless, untalented, waste of fucking space, almost ginger . . .

Chris   All right, mate.

Holly   I like this game. Do me. Do me.

Dev (*to* **Holly**)   Ok, low-class, drunken . . . beautiful, beautiful, beautiful . . .

Holly   Say that again I'll fucking deck ya.

Amy   It's our last night, can we stop with the insults?

They are all mock angry, but also laughing.

Chris   Shut up! You stupid cow!

They laugh.

Amy   Come here and say that, you scrawny ginger twat!

More laughter.

There is a knock at the door. **Dev** *answers it.*

Michael (*off; bad Spanish accent*)   Buenas noches. Room service?

Holly   Eh?

Michael *enters. He is formerly of athletic build, tall, well kept, expensively dressed in Orlebar Brown trousers, a fine linen shirt, Christian Louboutin loafers. In his hand he holds a bottle of expensive mineral water.*

Michael   Hello boys.

Chris   You made it.

Michael   You think I'd miss this, Chrissy? 547 Stairway to Heaven.

Chris (*referring to the mineral water*)   What's this?

Michael   I'm taking it easy, boss. Don't give me a hard time.

(*To* **Holly** *and* **Amy** – *extending hand*.) I'm Michael and these are my oldest friends.

Holly   We've heard all about you.

Michael   I've changed.

Amy   Amy.

Holly   Holly.

Michael (*shaking their hands*)   Lovely to meet you.

Dev   Where have you come from?

Michael   From the gods, from the hills, from a crush of gyrating bodies lost in a riff, but all the time I could hear a voice in my ear: 'Hotel Pantinos! Hotel Pantinos!' I thought it was on the track, but then the track changed and it was still there . . . Before I forget . . .

He hands **Chris** *a wrapped gift.*

Chris   What's this?

Michael   A little something . . .

The gift is their self-pressed single 'Out of Season' with a photo of them as a cover.

Chris   Where did you find this?

Michael   Tracked it down in Australia, bud. Might be the last.

Chris   Australia?

Michael   We sent it to a producer there – who's still alive – just.

Chris (*moved*)   Cheers, man.

They hug.

Michael   Bring it in, Dev.

Dev *joins – there is genuine affection.*

Holly *picks up the record.*

Holly   Awww, boys . . . you look so fresh.

Michael   Taken in this very room on my dad's Pentax – just by that wardrobe, which is still here!

Holly   Let's take one now.

Michael   Splendid.

Holly   Do exactly the same poses and everything.

Michael *hands* **Holly** *his phone.*

They go to the wardrobe and with consultation and bickering re-create the picture: **Michael** *side on, arms folded looking directly to camera,* **Chris** *to the left of the wardrobe, arms open looking expectantly towards* **Michael,** *and* **Dev** *to the right of the wardrobe, arms by his side looking at the ceiling.*

Holly *snaps away.*

Holly   Now do a stupid one.

Dev   That was a stupid one.

Holly   Pull faces or summat – go wild . . .

They all pull mad faces and poses.

Amy   So this was yer big hit?

Michael   I wouldn't go that far.

Amy   You gotta play it.

Michael   On what?

Holly   Can you not sing it or summat?

Michael   I don't remember the lyrics, do you?

Dev   Nah.

Chris   I do. I play it in my set sometimes.

He picks up his guitar and plays the intro.

Chris (*sings with raw feeling*)

'Out of Season'

It was raining
So I stayed in
The sky was grey and I was blue
But In my heart there . . .
There was a heatwave
And it's burning babe because of you

Well, I never check the weather
Just walk out without a coat
Sunshine, rain or wind whatever
Standing out here on my own

I'm out of season
And you're the reason
I'm always freezing on a summer's day
Since you breezed into my life
The clouds have gathered
And it's looking like they're here to stay

Round and round and round we go
Like back at school we're eight years old
I will be there for you
Try to make it through the rain
We missed the bus, we caught the train
I will be there for you

So will you teach me
How to reach you
Standing out here in the rain
The April showers don't distract me
From feeling all this pain

Well, I never check the weather
Just walk out against the cold
Sunshine, rain and wind can't touch me
They say that I'm young, but all I'm feeling is old

I'm out of season
And you're the reason
I'm always freezing on a summer's day
Since you walked out of my life
The clouds have gathered
And it's looking like they're here to stay

Round and round and round we go
The years go by, but we don't know
I will be there for you
Times move on, but we don't change
The youth today they seem so strange
I will be there for you

Memories of yesterday
I still hold on, don't walk away
Oh yeah . . . I will be there for you
When all is said and done, my friend
I'll be with you until the end
Oh yeah, I will be there for you

I'm out of season (it's raining)
I'm out of season (it's freezing)
I'm out of season
I'm out of season.

During the song:

Dev *drums on a suitcase and pitches in with backing vocals.*

Amy *also pitches in with backing vocals and harmonies.*

Holly *might sing, but also dance wildly, losing herself in the melody.*

At this point a soundtrack might also be overlaid with strings and there might be lights so, for a brief moment they are the indie super-band they could have been.

At some point **Michael** *takes over the lead vocals, loving it, showing off.*

At the end of the song, they laugh and embrace. **Michael** *clinches* **Holly** *–* **Dev** *clocks this.*

Holly   That was a banger.

Michael   I guess I did know the words!

Chris (*to* **Dev**)   That was me and you wrote that in this very room.

Dev   I remember. I do remember.

Holly   It was brilliant.

Michael   No, you are brilliant. You are a sensational mover.

Holly   D'ya reckon?

Michael   I'm always looking for great movers for my artists, for their videos.

Holly   Yeah?

Michael   We should talk.

Holly   We are talking.

Michael   We should talk some more.

Beat.

Dev (*to* **Michael**)   So where the fuck have you been?

Michael   Sorry?

Dev   You're six days late – where have you been?

Michael   No, you said where the fuck have you been?

Dev   I just want to know where you've been?

Michael   Long story, bud. Long and boring.

Dev   Go on

Michael   LA, baby!

Dev   Of course!

Michael   Friday afternoon. I'm set. Holdall under the desk, a little over-excited, when I get a call.

Chris   Who from?

Michael   Can't say. NDA'ed up to the eyeballs, but if I say my colleagues would sacrifice their children for a sit-down with this person, you might get my drift. Next thing I'm in a car. Next thing I am in his Malibu mansion playing ping pong.

Chris   Ping pong?

Michael   Table tennis – turns out this is how he likes to conduct business. So we play: I win, he wins, I win, he wins, and while we play we talk about the deal, but also everything else: the environment, God, Trump. We play for a whole day and then I tell him I have a friend's birthday in Ibiza. He says this will be the final game . . . We play, we're neck and neck, and then on the final point, the decider, he delivers an unplayable backhand smash, but I instinctively catch it on the volley and win. Next thing I'm on his private jet, letter of agreement in hand . . . *et voilà*!

Amy   If you think that's boring come work for Network Rail.

Michael   I'm sure it has its moment.

Amy   Not many, though we did have an away day to Bridlington.

Michael   LA's not all it's cracked up to be.

Amy   Neither is Bridlington.

Michael *laughs.*

Dev   So, you've been here since Tuesday?

Michael   Eh?

Dev   If you got the call on Friday, flew out to LA on Saturday, played table tennis Sunday, then flew here from LA on Monday . . .

Michael   Well, yes . . . I had some business with Mr David Drexler.

Chris   Where's he now?

Michael   At the other place.

Holly   What place?

Chris   It's called Yorks. It's in the hills.

Holly   We know Yorks. We got in on a day pass last year, except Amy didn't like it.

Chris   Why not?

Amy   Cos it were up itself.

Michael (*laughing*)   Too right. It used to be cool when Elton had his parties there, but these days it's infinity pools and luxury restaurants. That's not rock 'n' roll. That's Saga. Plus everyone was off their faces on Charlie and I'm not doing that.

Dev   Since when?

Michael   Since I took stock of my life, asked myself what's important. Yorks isn't. It's nothing, it's money, there's no beauty, no magic. No, those things are here in this very room where we had fun, didn't we? Back when youth glowed from our faces, no money, but we had . . . everything. And we're going to have it again. Tonight, boys and girls, it's here – just like in the old days, baby! Come on!

Chris   Shall I make you a Rula Lenska?

Michael   A what?

Chris   Whisky, tonic, dash of orange.

Michael   Sounds disgusting.

Chris   You invented it cos Prof picked up tonic instead of ginger ale.

Michael   Must have been desperate.

Chris   Honestly, it tastes ok.

He goes off to make the drink; the others indicate that it's disgusting.

Michael   Just a small one, bud. I'm pacing myself.

He surveys the room.

So, this is where it all happened . . . feels different.

Chris (*from the bathroom*)   It's a deluxe room now, pal.

Michael   That's depressing.

He clocks the wardrobe.

Hang on . . . didn't we . . . lock you in there?

Dev   Yes.

Michael   Forgive me – I was a cunt.

Chris   That's not all you did in there, mate.

Michael   What? . . . Oh shit!

Michael *and* **Chris** *laugh.*

Holly   Tell all.

Michael   No. No. No. No. No. No.

The next few lines can overlap.

Chris   First night we were here we met two ladies from Doncaster . . .

Michael   Shut up!

Chris   . . . brought 'em back here . . .

Michael   Oi!

Chris   . . . and Michael took his into the wardrobe.

Michael   It wasn't like that.

Chris   It was exactly like that.

Holly   What did you do in the wardrobe?

Chris   Use yer imagination.

Michael   No, we only went in there cos Dev wouldn't leave the room.

Chris (*laughing*)   That was it.

Michael   Chris took his into the bathroom, but Dev insisted he wasn't going anywhere, so . . .

Holly   You shagged her in the wardrobe?

Michael   It would have been awkward if he was tucked up in bed next to us.

Chris   Having a wank.

Amy   Awkward for her anyway, I'd say.

Michael   I am not proud of it.

Dev   You are kind of boasting though.

Holly   So you just stayed here while they . . .?

Dev   No, I went for a walk. Along the beach. Alone.

Holly   Awwww.

Dev   Please don't make that sound.

Michael (*to* **Dev**)   To be fair you were never exactly a ladies' man.

Dev   I was ok.

Michael   I thought you were hot stuff, bud. I'd have done you.

Chris   You did everyone else.

Michael   No, you did, or tried to.

Chris   Shut up!

Michael (*indicating* **Dev**)   But, this one . . . special case.

Amy   How so?

Michael   An old soul shall we say? Remember the first time we saw him?

Chris   Can I forget? First day at uni – there was a student look – spiky hair, drainpipe jeans . . .

Holly   What jeans?

Chris   Skinny . . . kind of.

Michael   . . . goths, some metal fans, Pradev Banarjee rocks up in a tweed jacket and cravat.

Dev   It was a scarf.

Chris   Don't forget the hat.

Michael   And a fedora with a feather in it.

Holly   A what?

Chris   One of them Indiana Jones hats.

Amy   Sounds stylish.

Dev   I was.

Chris   And a tiny bit camp.

Michael   Professor Pradev we christened him, Professor P because he looked like a professor – and a homosexual – which was cool.

Dev   Why are you smirking then?

Michael   If you were gay I'd welcome you with open arms

Dev   Still smirking.

Michael (*tickling* **Dev**)   Come out. Come out – wherever you are.

They all laugh.

Dev   Does emasculating me make you feel more virile?

Michael   I'm kidding, buddy. Kidding. Can't you take a joke?

Chris (*presenting drink*)   I give you: the Rula Lenska –
created in this very room, Hotel Pantinos, 1995.

Michael (*takes the drink*)   To us, dear friends of thirty years
and you ladies who I've just met . . . this is what it's about,
good times with beautiful people. To friendship. To beauty.
To happy memories.

He drinks, grimaces.

Though I reckon some things are best left in the past.

They all laugh.

Michael   Music!

Chris   I'll play us something.

Michael   No, bud, I'll stick something on Spotify.

*He grabs his phone and plays fast-paced dance music – the track we
heard at the beginning of the scene.*

*He dances. His moves are not as cool as he thinks, but he uses them
to pull in **Holly** and **Amy**.*

*Seeing this **Dev** joins the dance trying to engage **Holly**.*

*The track gets more frenetic as **Michael** and **Dev** up their moves,
competing for **Holly**'s attention.*

Amy *dances alone.* **Chris** *joins her.*

They get into twerking – the game becomes: show us your best twerk.
Amy *is stylish,* **Chris** *is pneumatic,* **Michael** *is blatant,* **Holly** *is
sexy and* **Dev** *is a tad unhinged as he proffers his arse cheeks
towards* **Holly**.

Michael *slaps* **Dev**'s *arse cheek really hard.*

Dev *howls in pain and walks off.*

The others stop dancing. **Michael** *turns the music off.*

Michael   What's up?

Dev   Nothing.

Holly   Is it yer back?

Dev   No.

Holly   It's not your tat is it?

Michael   His what?

Holly   He got a tattoo.

Chris   On his arse.

Michael   Let's have a look.

Dev   No.

Michael   I will pull your pants down.

Dev (*gingerly revealing his arse cheek*)   I think I got sand in it.

He now reveals a badly written 'I love Dvorak'.

Michael   'I love Anorak'?

Dev   Dvořák. He's a composer.

Michael   What brought this on?

Dev   The New World Symphony.

Holly (*laughing*)   We were off our faces and I dared him.

Michael *and* **Chris** *fall about laughing.*

Dev   It doesn't look like 'Anorak', does it?

Holly   It won't when it heals.

Chris   Else get a walking boot on the other cheek say you're into hiking.

Michael   The two peaks challenge.

Chris, **Michael** *and* **Holly** *laugh.*

Dev   I'm going to give it a pat down with a warm flannel.

He goes into the bathroom.

Chris, **Michael** *and* **Holly** *continue laughing.*

Amy   Guys – lay off him.

Michael   She's right. Don't make Dev the butt of our jokes.

They laugh.

Chris   Enough of your toilet humour.

They laugh.

Holly   That's a bum joke.

They laugh.

Amy (*to* **Holly**)   You lay off him too.

Holly   We're only having a laff.

Michael *puts on some dance music.*

Michael   This is a client of mine – played Coachella last year.

Chris   Nice.

He grabs his guitar and jams with the music.

Michael *dances with* **Holly***, twirling her around in a salsa style. While dancing he also whispers stuff in her ear. She laughs.*

Dev *comes out of the toilet and, seeing them twirling, takes some pics on his phone, which they pose for.*

Amy *comes over to* **Dev***.*

Michael (*to* **Chris**)   Do you know what, buddy – the way you sang earlier . . . goosebumps.

Chris   Cheers.

Michael   This is what I'm talking to Dave Drex about.

Chris   All they want is youth.

Michael   Fifty is the new thirty, mate.

Chris   Do you honestly think he'll consider me?

Michael   I'm fighting your corner.

(*To* **Holly**.) We were famous once.

Holly   I heard.

Michael   Got played by John Peel.

Chris   And interest from Q Prime off the back of it.

Michael   Funnily enough I was laughing with the Q Prime boys about that the other day.

Holly   It's a shame you packed it in.

Michael   Our drummer left. Got a scholarship to study abroad.

Holly   Get a new drummer.

Chris   Dev and me wrote the songs . . . me and Michael tried to after, but they weren't great . . .

Michael   What you on about? 'I want to be your vagina' was a much-maligned lyric

Holly   Shame though. Could ya not have re-formed when he was back?

Michael   Missed our moment. In this business you've got to seize those babies.

Holly   What were you called again?

Michael   Frampton Sound Experience.

Chris   Experiment.

Michael   Yes! My parents lived in Frampton in Dorset. Nothing to do with the band. Just liked the name.

Chris   I loved that place. Old Manor House – built in the 1500s. The doors were like genuine Elizabethan, like being in a film or summat.

Holly   Would you have had me in yer band?

Michael   If we had we might have got somewhere.

Dev   Not necessarily.

Holly   Rude.

Michael   Ouch.

Dev   Like he said, we missed our moment.

Michael   With a voice and face like that we might have had other moments.

Dev   Or she might have left us for another band. It's a fickle business. Bowie was in three bands before he settled on The Spiders from Mars. I was telling Penny that. You know . . . your daughter Penny. I bumped into her in a bar in East London. Gave her a lift home.

Michael   She said.

Dev   We had a good chat. She sent me some of her tracks after – interesting I thought.

Michael   That's why you do what you do and I'm a music agent.

Holly   She does music too?

Michael   She calls it that.

Dev   I think she's good.

Michael   Who wants champagne?

Chris/Holly   Yes!

Dev   What I like about Penny is there's no bullshit. She has strong views, but didn't we all?

Michael   Difference is I didn't have everything on a plate.

Dev   You grew up in a Tudor mansion in Dorset. Your dad was the CEO of a bank.

Michael   I don't bite the hand that feeds me.

Dev   We talked about men . . . the patriarchy.

Michael *laughs.*

Dev   She's young – isn't that when you're supposed to be angry? – We were, about Thatcher, capitalism . . . Some of our songs were protest songs remember? Remember how we used to go hunting for the best raves and the police would come and bust them up – that was a protest of sorts against what we were told was normal, acceptable. No, I enjoyed talking to Penny – she's bright and her anger seems apt.

Michael   How many bottles?

Holly   Five.

Amy (*to* **Michael**)   Thought you were off booze.

Michael   For my best bud's birthday.

Dev   Plus I reckon she's got a point, people like you have fucked the world.

Michael   Oh yeah?

Dev   White, middle-aged, entitled . . . Fucked the music business at least.

Michael   How have I done that then?

Dev   You go on about beauty and artists, but you don't care for art . . . and what is beauty to you if you can't monetise it. Beauty's a meal deal, art's a bottomless drink. You take what's innocent and honestly wrought and you turn it into shit.

Beat.

Dev   I'm kidding, mate. Kidding. Can't you take a joke?

Holly   I think the world is fucked. I think we're all fucked.

Michael   That's why we need booze.

Dev   No, I have time for Penny. I like her.

Michael   Have her.

Dev   I could have.

Beat.

Michael   What?

Dev   I'm kidding, mate. Kidding. I felt protective, paternal actually. I always wanted a daughter. There she was, drunk, skirt up to her bum, laughing, but anyone could see she's a bit lost. She needs love and guidance I reckon. You know she's started texting me just to ask me random shit. I don't mind. I text her back. Shall I send her that picture of you dancing?

Michael   No. (*Takes* **Dev***'s phone and tosses it on the bed, then picks up the hotel phone.*) Room service . . . I want champagne . . . Room 547 . . . what have you got? Bollinger? Clicquot? . . . No. 1 Premium . . . what's that, never heard of it . . . that's the best? . . . Right. Send up five bottles . . . Thirty minutes? Where are you getting it from, France? . . . I know there's an event on, but we're gasping . . . No, I am not coming down – it's called room service – the clue is in the name . . . Look, bring it up now and I'll give you a decent tip. Five bottles, yeah? Make them magnums . . . magnums . . . no not fucking ice creams – magnums, big bottles, magnums, are you a fucking moron?

Amy   Classy guy your friend.

Chris   He's a mover and shaker.

Michael   . . . Just bring five bottles. I'll pay cash.

Dev   He's been moving in on our girlfriends for as long as I can remember.

Michael   Don't need to, mate – they come to me.

Dev   Of course.

Michael   To be honest it was painful to watch – how you could never seal a deal.

Dev   So you'd seal it for me.

Michael   Perhaps you never wanted to – with a woman – that's my theory.

Dev   And my theory is you don't even like women – you only like the power you have over them. That's why you struggle with Penny, because she doesn't give you her power.

Chris   Rein it in, mate.

Dev   It's true though, isn't it?

Chris   This is our one night together.

Dev   . . . it was true then . . . with Laura.

Michael   Who?

Dev   The Doncaster girl.

Michael   He actually remembers her name.

Dev   You weren't interested in her.

Michael   I can't remember anything about her to be honest.

Dev   I can . . . because I got talking to her first – her and her friend, Cath. You guys had gone off for a beer and me and her were getting on quite well till you came and swooped.

Michael (*laughing*)   Are you honestly still pissed off about what happened thirty years ago?

Chris (*laughing*)   Let it go, mate. (*Miming quotation marks.*) 'All is fair in love and war'?

Michael (*laughing*)   Plus 'She didn't fancy you'?

Dev   No, that bit was ok, but it was how you then pursued her all week, told her you were into her, while telling us you thought she was an ugly pig . . .

Michael   Right . . . Shut up.

Dev   You don't even like women – that's what Penny thinks.

Michael   You're getting over-excited, dear.

Dev   It's about power.

Michael   You know what happens when you get over-excited.

Dev   Try it.

Michael   Shall we go get this champagne, Holly?

Dev   You can't stop yourself.

Michael   Have a little bop?

Dev   And your daughter hasn't talked to you in how long?

Michael (*to* **Chris**)   Right, grab his legs.

Michael *grabs* **Dev** *who struggles.* **Chris** *hesitates.*

Michael   Come on, Chrissy!

Laughing, **Chris** *and* **Michael** *grab* **Dev** *who protests, albeit laughing.* **Holly** *joins in the fun.*

Michael   Shall we goose him, Holly, shall we?

Holly   Yeah, let's!

Dev   Get off me.

Michael   It's the wardrobe for you, my boy.

Amy   What you doing?

Michael   When he gets excited we put him in the wardrobe.

They bundle **Dev** *in the wardrobe and* **Michael** *locks it.*

Amy   Let him out of there.

Michael   No.

Chris   It's just a bit of fun.

Amy   Doesn't look like fun.

Dev *kicks and screams in the wardrobe.*

Amy   You're going too far.

Holly   It's funny.

Amy   You're tekking it too far.

Michael   It's for his own good.

He knocks on the wardrobe door.

Dev? You ok? You calm? Cos I can't let you out until you are.

Chris   So stop kicking and screaming and calm down.

Dev *stops kicking and screaming.*

Michael   Good.

He opens the wardrobe. As **Dev** *emerges,* **Michael** *shoves him back violently. A thud.* **Michael** *grabs an open bottle of cava, shakes it up and sprays* **Dev***, then closes and locks the door again.*

Michael   Come on! That was funny.

Chris   My clothes could have been in there.

Amy   What the fuck?!

Michael   Don't worry, the real stuff is on its way.

Amy   You are a prick. I knew that from the minute you walked in – flashing yer charm and yer LA stories. I could see right through you.

(*To* **Holly**.) And you ought to see right through him too cos a fella like that has no respect. Like those tossers in that Yorks place. Think they're special, think they're better than us. Don't say it, but you know it. Have nothing but contempt in their souls – and money of course – lots of that, but I reckon they ain't that special and I reckon everyone deserves respect. So let him out of there now.

Michael   No.

Holly   Yeah, let him out.

Michael   I don't want to.

Amy (*to* **Chris**)   Are you going to let him do this to your friend?

Chris   Why are you getting so heavy?

Amy   I won't ask again.

Michael   What are you going to do about it?

Amy   I've learned a trick or two in my career.

Michael   Network Rail?

Amy   Before that I was a healthcare assistant on mental health wards. Fifteen years. Sometimes we'd deal with men much bigger than you so manic they didn't know their own strength. Occasionally when they lost it – to save yourself – what you do are some quick hard jabs to the throat or some other vulnerable area then . . .

She takes a bottle of cava.

. . . a strong violent jut up their arse and you know what . . . I've seen those guys crumple on the floor after that, I've seen them whimper like kids, like little dogs . . .

Michael   Think you can take me?

Amy (*deadly serious now*)   I'll give it a good fucking go.

For a beat we feel things might escalate.

Michael   Charming, but what I'd really like to know is where this champagne has got to.

He sits down and gets out a wrap of cocaine and starts to chop out some lines.

Chris   Don't mind him. Gets excitable.

Amy *unlocks the wardrobe.*

Amy   You alright, luv?

Dev   Yeah.

She helps **Dev** *out, dishevelled and wet.*

Amy Holly and I are going downstairs, you wanna come?

Chris Hang on –

Dev No, I'm going to clean up.

Amy You sure?

Dev Yeah . . . Thank you.

He goes into the bathroom.

Holly Are we really going?

Amy Yeah.

Holly But we're going home . . . this is our last night!

Amy Let's leave these *boys* to it.

Holly *now hovers by the bathroom door.*

Amy You should think about your friends, Chris.

Chris What about them?

Amy Know who they are.

Chris I do.

Amy (*to* **Holly**) Let's go.

Holly Dev! Do you want me to stay?

Amy Come on.

Holly . . . I only meant for it to be fun. I only meant . . .

Amy You are enough, Chris. You just don't know that you are.

Amy *leaves.* **Holly** *hovers.*

Holly (*to* **Chris**) . . . Are you not going after her?

Chris Why should I?

Holly Cos you and her . . .

Chris   Bit dramatic. Maybe that's why her biker fella left her.

Holly   Who, Mark?

Chris   Yeah. (*To* **Michael**.) Escaped down M62 on his Kawasaki.

Holly   No. He came off his Kawasaki on the M62, Chris. They were engaged.

She leaves.

Chris *goes to the door – he wants to follow.*

Michael   Fancy a toot?

Chris   I thought you weren't doing that.

Michael   I'm not really – did a couple earlier. This is part two of your birthday present, bud.

Chris *is still at the door.*

Michael   The redhead's fire. Bit mouthy, but I'll tell you what . . .

Chris   What?

Michael   I know what would shut her up.

Chris *is silent.*

Michael   The other one's fit but a bit vacuous.

Chris   Why do you . . .

Michael   What?

Chris   . . . go too far?

Michael   I know. Oops!

He does a line.

Tell you what, bud . . . there's a party in the hills.

Chris   Yorks?

Michael   Fuck Yorks. This is a friend of mine's villa. Pleasure palace and when I say pleasure I mean any . . . thing – drugs, booze, girls . . . Oh my lord! Girls . . . these girls . . . I'm talking proper . . . I'm talking you will need a barrow to wheel your boner around.

Chris   What about Dev?

Michael   It's our last night in Ibiza, mate.

Beat.

I told Dave Drex you'd be there.

Dev *comes out from the bathroom.*

Michael   Here he is. How are you, buddy?

Dev   Wet.

Michael *laughs.* **Dev** *laughs too.*

Michael   Sorry, bud. Couldn't help myself.

Chris   To be fair it kinda had to happen for old time's sake.

Michael   How was it in there this time?

Dev   Great. Time to think.

Michael   Silver lining.

Dev   I met the twenty-year-old me in there – had a little chat.

Michael   Speaking to yourself?

Dev   No, he was actually there cowering so I reached out and told him it was ok.

Michael   Right . . .

Dev   Told him he was dressed fine. At least he didn't look ordinary.

Michael   Certainly didn't, bud.

Dev   Told him to walk away from you because that's an abusive relationship being set up there and it's going to play out over thirty-one years, a life sentence. Told him some people you know are bad for you so steer clear, but some end up hiding in plain sight.

Michael   Starting to sound a bit strange now.

Dev   But we also laughed at you getting on his side whenever he turns up because you have so little confidence in yourself, or kidding yourself that he will ever help you in the music business, that's funny, your self-delusion is hilarious, but the biggest joke was me running away to the other side of the world when we could have made it.

Chris   What?

Dev   There was no scholarship in America. I ran away because of this . . . Oh, and that nickname Professor P.

Michael   What about it?

Dev   That didn't start off as Pradev, did it?

Michael   What are you talking about?

Dev   Your harmless little Asian friend, the one you both laugh at so you can feel a tiny bit taller . . . Good old Professor P . . . Good old Professor Paki.

Michael   Please don't.

Dev   I wonder, was it the Tudor mansion you grew up in, built, no doubt, on the bones of slaves?

Michael   He's going back to Tudor times now.

Dev   Why not?

Michael   Too far, bud. Just go back and figure out why you don't feel good.

Dev   Is that your best advice?

Michael People like you always want to find someone to blame – now it's the patriarchy, now it's identity – does it occur to you, it's actually about you. You don't feel good – that's no one's fault. I never called you Professor Paki, but even if I had, it as practically a term of endearment back then, not some massive racist slur.

Dev To be fair I played my part. I let you say those things.

Michael Finally, some recognition, some ownership.

Dev If you want to talk about ownership, we can.

Michael What do you mean?

Dev Do you really not know or do you just not want to?

Michael You know what – I'll leave this for you and your university forums or Penny and her mates whose pronouns I always fuck up . . . but if you think it's been easy for me, you're wrong. We all have hills to climb, they make us who we are. But you, my daughter and the perennial whingers want it easy.

Dev You think it's easy for her?

Michael Cancel me – blame me – you won't feel any better. It'll be something else that gets you down – who will you blame then? No, you need to take a good look at yourself.

Dev You first, bud.

Michael I'm alright as it happens.

Dev Yeah?

Michael Are we done?

Dev One last thing – for Penny and little Dev.

He slaps **Michael** *hard across the face with an open hand.*
Michael *recoils shocked.*

Then **Michael** *springs up and twists* **Dev***'s arm behind his back.*
Chris *tries to stop him but* **Michael** *pushes* **Dev** *against the bed
and twists his arm.*

Chris   Let go of him, mate.

Michael   You ever hit me again I will break your arm.

Chris   Lay off him!

Michael   You gonna make me?

Chris   If I have to.

Michael *lets go of* **Dev***, who turns and holds his arm.*

Michael   He made me do it. Wound me up as usual. Look,
I'm not an arsehole. Ok, I am, but I'm also your friend. I've
known you for thirty years – you can't just . . . I drove across
the island to see you.

Chris   Eventually.

Michael   You are my friends. My oldest friends. I love you
guys.

Dev   But it's not love, is it? What is it? Control? Contempt?
Because that is what it feels like – contempt for us, for
yourself probably, and for Penny.

Michael   What the fuck do you know about Penny?

Dev   Only this . . . that you are lucky, so lucky to have a
brilliant, articulate, intelligent . . . to have brought her into
the world . . . to have the closest connection with that person
and for them to have that with you . . . that is meaning . . .
that must be wonderful . . . and I would be proud, so proud
if I had someone like that in my life. I'd value her deeply. I
wouldn't run away. I wouldn't push her away.

Michael   How dare you lecture me! You don't know what
it's like. You don't know anything. I made sure that girl had
the best education, the best of everything – I have given her
everything, but it's not enough. They all want it handed to
them on a plate. She's been spoiled and I have watched it

happen. You don't know what it's like having your child
turned against you – how could you? You don't have kids.
You've never even had a proper girlfriend for fuck's sake
because no one would have you, because you haven't got it
in you, either of you. So stick to what you're good at – you
with your poncy books that no one reads, you with your
empty gigs in shitty pubs. You're shit. You're nothing. You're
a pair of fucking losers.

Beat.

Listen . . . let's just . . . what a night! Let's start again. Let's
go to this other bash, take some pills, dance it off. We'll laugh
about this one day. The night it all went pear-shaped in
Ibiza. Come on, it's our last night – thirty years! It's not
going to end like this.

Beat.

Chrissy . . . come on, it's your birthday! Chrissy!

Beat.

What, you just gonna send me off on my own?

Beat.

Ok. What'll I tell Dave Drexler?

Chris Tell him I'm playing the King's Head, Newington
next Tuesday if he wants to come down.

Michael *leaves.*

Chris *sits on chair.* **Dev** *sits on the bed nursing his arm.*

Perhaps some Dvořák overlaid with a dance track.

Scene Two

The same. Late morning.

The wardrobe door is slightly ajar.

Dev's *right arm is in a makeshift sling. In his good hand he holds
his toiletry bag.*

His oversized suitcase is open on the floor.

Chris *is on his phone.*

They are both in their own worlds.

Chris   Taxi's on its way.

Beat.

Do you want some rolls?

Dev   We missed breakfast.

Chris   I know, but I've seen where they leave them in cling film with them little packets of jam and shit.

Dev *shakes his head.*

Beat.

Chris's *phone pings. He looks at it and texts back.*

Chris   It's that bird from choir – another picture of her tied up . . . in an allotment this time.

Beat.

Michael says he's been trying to text you. Just wants to know you're ok.

Beat.

Dev   I'm done, Chris. I've walked away.

Beat.

Holly *is at the door.*

Holly   Heya!

Dev   Hey!

Holly   All packed?

Dev   Yeah.

Chris   I'll get these rolls.

He leaves.

Holly   What the fuck happened to you?

Dev   You should have seen the other guy.

Holly   That sling's shit. Come here.

She rearranges the sling.

Dev   You should have been a nurse.

Holly   I was once . . . kinda.

Holly *takes the bag out of* **Dev**'s *hand.*

Holly   What goes in here?

Dev   Toiletries.

She goes into the bathroom.

Holly   There's nowt left in here.

Dev   I know.

She comes out of the bathroom.

Holly   How you gonna manage with all this stuff?

Dev   Porter?

Holly   I don't think they have 'em.

Beat.

I were thinking about Robbie's Tina Turner costume – it were kinda shit.

Dev   It wasn't about the costume per se.

Holly   Per what?

Dev   Someone said something to me at the bar. I reacted.

Holly   What did they say?

Dev   Got any curry.

Holly   Who said that?

Dev   Some guy.

Holly   Why would you have curry?

Dev   For emergencies?

Holly   Is that why you wouldn't sing?

Dev   And also because I wouldn't have wanted women to leave their husbands.

Beat.

My voice is like Krishna's flute, it attracts random females from miles around.

Holly   Chris's what?

Dev   It's a Hindu reference.

Holly   I don't get about 30 per cent of what you say.

Beat.

You gonna come visit me in Hull?

Dev   Sure.

Holly   Meet the kids.

Dev   Love to.

Holly   Just got to get Ryan's ADHD under control and Rianne's court case sorted.

Dev   Saying that it gets very busy during term time.

Holly *smiles: He does too.*

Beat.

Dev   Would you . . . sit on my suitcase?

Holly   Well there's an offer.

Dev   While I close it.

Holly   You sit on it – I'll close it.

Dev *sits on the suitcase while she closes it.*

Dev   If I came to Hull . . . and we . . . I'd doubt everything, you know, you, your kids, the age difference, the distance, whether it's viable, whether we're suited . . . I'd be in a world of doubt, *but that is all about me* . . . I've never been able to let someone in . . . not really . . . and what I need . . . is someone who can tolerate my doubt, self-doubt I should say . . . who can put up with it . . . with whom I can surrender . . . learn to surrender . . . day by day, hour by hour . . .

Holly   How does this lock work?

Dev   I think you press it in at the sides.

Beat.

Dev   I guess what I'm saying is . . . I'm a nightmare, but I'm not a bad guy.

Holly *kisses him tenderly.*

Dev   What was that?

Holly   Dunno.

Chris *is back.* **Dev** *is whistling quietly.*

Chris   Sorry . . .

Holly (*picking up* **Dev**'*s case*)   You're okay.

Dev   I can do that.

Holly   I don't think you can. Bring the ruck.

She takes the case and is on her way out.

Chris   Is Amy around?

Holly   She went on that boat trip.

Chris   Ah.

Holly   She liked you.

She goes.

Beat.

Chris   I got you a roll.

Dev   I said I didn't want one.

Chris   There was Nutella.

Beat.

I never called you that name you know – Professor . . . He did, but I never did.

Beat.

Chris   I am sorry though.

Beat.

If we'd carried on writing songs we could have been Pradev and Pringle like Lennon McCartney – Pradev Pringle . . .

Dev   Sounds like estate agents.

Chris (*broken*)   Dev . . . don't walk away from me.

Dev   Better get this taxi.

Dev *is on his way out.*

Chris   I've got your disease by the way.

Dev   What's that?

Chris   Had a dream last night: I was in this field somewhere – don't know where exactly. I think it might be near the Wolds . . . near my auntie up around Kirby Grindalythe. Me dad used to take us there to see my cousins, to play in the fields behind the willows . . . It's night. There's a moon and it's really low and it's not lighting up much. The field's dark, but not pitch, and there are a couple of children running around. Just them and me. And every now and then I catch a glimpse of their faces where the moonlight has reached and they're . . . beautiful. Not like pretty, but in the way they made me feel. And they stop for a second and I think they're aware I'm there. And I go towards them. I feel drawn towards them but I can't get near. They're there and I'm close but I can't reach them. And they start crying but I still can't find them. They want me to, but I can't. It's fucking unbearable. (*Beat.*) Got the number of that therapist?

Dev   Sure.

Phone pings.

Chris   I'll be down in a minute.

Dev *makes to go.*

Chris   And would you tell Holly to tell Amy goodbye.

Dev *nods and goes.*

Chris *takes the guitar and puts it in the wardrobe.*

As he does, the wardrobe door swings widely ajar to reveal an unfathomable depth of murk, at once terrifying, yet also beguiling, almost beautiful.

Phone pings.

Chris *sits on the bed.*

He gazes into the wardrobe with wonder and terror.

Blackout.

For a complete listing of
Methuen Drama titles, visit:
www.bloomsbury.com/drama

Follow us on Twitter and keep up to date
with our news and publications
@MethuenDrama